CW00617600

DOGSBODIES

Creative Fitness for Canines

by
Judith Wills
and
Dominic Poelsma

Souvenir Press

Copyright©2000 by Judith Wills and Dominic Poelsma

The right of Judith Wills to be identified as author and of
Dominic Poelsma to be identified as illustrator of this work has
been asserted by them in accordance with the Copyright,
Designs and Patents Act 1988.

First Published by
Souvenir Press Ltd.
43 Great Russell Street, London WC1B 3PA

All Rights Reserved. No part of this publication may be
reproduced, stored in a retrieval system, or transmitted, in any
form or by any means, electronic, mechanical, photocopying,
recording or otherwise without the prior permission of the
Copyright owner.

ISBN 0 285 63577 8

Typeset by
Photoprint, Torquay
Printed in Great Britain by the
University Press, Cambridge

Contents

Introduction

You love your dog no matter what size he is or what shape he is in – of course you do.

But canine health and fitness are important, and to be taken seriously. A third of the seven million or so dogs in this country are fat, and another third (not necessarily the *same* third) are unfit.

This is the book for people who feel they may know – or even own – such a dog and who wish to improve their understanding of the canine psyche, and therefore their technique and tact in dealing with personal pet fitness to achieve the desired results.

In other words, in DOGSBODIES you will discover how to reduce your dog's calorie intake and increase his exercise output while avoiding all manner of possible problems and hitherto undreamed-of levels of recalcitrance which you might otherwise encounter. If access to food were to suddenly seriously diminish and 'walkies' were to take on a whole new, marathon-type meaning without warning, 'war' might not be too strong a term for what could ensue in the health-challenged canine household.

We aim to show that you need not be daunted by the task in hand – *any* out of shape dog, yes *any* out of shape dog can become fitter and live a long, happy and healthy life.

The secrets of persuading him to do so without pain on either side are here within. . .

Chapter One

How does your dog shape up?

Some breeds, such as Clumbers and King Charles spaniels, tend to be less active and put on weight more easily than other breeds. Labradors are especially renowned for scavenging and general gluttony. All these dogs are *endomorph* types.

Ectomorphs like Salukis and whippets are prone to picky eating and may also be hyperactive. They are unlikely to cause you fitness worries but some may need specialist therapy from time to time.

Some dogs can eat a lot without gaining an ounce. These are very active, adventurous, forward-going dogs such as the Afghan.

Mesomorph types such as Rottweilers, Boxers, Great Danes and Bulldogs come naturally strong, muscular and sporty. They tend, however, to put on weight – and may possibly show signs of pent-up aggression – if they are denied enough regular vigorous exercise.

Many dogs put on weight as they get older and less active and their metabolic rate is slowing down. This rate can sometimes be speeded up with suitable encouragement.

There are several ways to tell if your dog is too fat.

Measure his waist circumference. If it is greater than his length from nose to tail, he is overweight. With a calculator to hand, you can be more specific. Divide his length by his waist circumference. If the resultant figure is under 0.75, he is obese. If it is 0.75–1.0, he is fat. 1–1.5 equals average, 1.5–2.0 equals slim, and 2.0 and over is too slim.

24 OVER 38 = 0.63

Does he wobble when he walks?

Does his belly touch the floor?

Can you pinch an inch or more of flesh
under his rib cage? Dare you try?

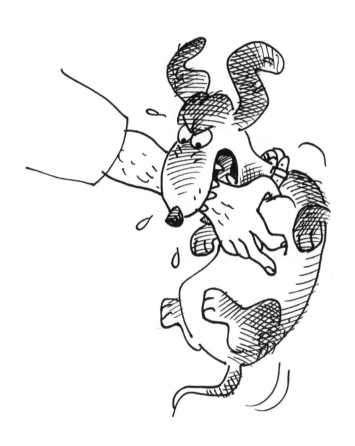

Be sure your dog really IS fat. He may just have a very thick coat. . .

. . . Underneath, he may be nice and slim.

How is his fitness? Does he have an inappropriate fear of exercise? Get the vet to look him over. Then try the Perceived Exertion Test (The PET test). Take him to a park; measure out a flat 100 metres and get him to run the 100 metres while you time him. It may be advisable here to have a helper hold him while you walk to the finish and call your pet. Check your results below.

1. Didn't move - assume he is very unfit.
2. Couldn't complete the distance – assume he is unfit.
3. Over 60 seconds – unfit unless a legitimate distraction arose during the test.
4. Around 30 seconds – okay for dogs with short legs.
5. 15 seconds or less – assume he is fit.

"unless a legitimate distraction arose . . ."

So he is overweight or not as fit as he could be? Don't worry – simple measures will soon get him shaped up.

Chapter Two

Your dog's diet

Most dogs enjoy fatty cuts of meat. If your dog is overweight, these should be restricted as much as possible.

You need to find other tasty protein sources for him instead. Low fat proteins include venison, pheasant, kangaroo, ostrich, lobster and caviare. Most owners are surprisingly willing to make sacrifices for the sake of their pet's health.

One tip to keep a hungry dog satisfied is to give him butcher's meat bones. This saves both calories and expense. Bones also provide occupational therapy – a must for any dog on a diet. He may even like to bury his bone, if you have a suitable place.

Rather than cutting down on the number of meals your dog has, it may be best simply to use portion control. Bulk up the dish for a hungry dog with low-calorie items. You can train your dog to enjoy vegetables. It helps to get him used to a wide variety of foods as early in his life as possible. In later years, he may be resistant to new things.

However, if you have been giving your dog more than two meals a day, you should consider reducing the number of mealtimes as well.

One main cause of obesity in dogs is their liking for between-meal snacks and treats. He doesn't actually need these titbits – and you don't need to give them, either. What you really both need is lots of hugs and affection.

Be ruthless and never feed your dog titbits from the meal table. It is best to ban him completely from the dining area. If necessary, shut him in another room. In this case you may need a set of earplugs.

To help him miss food less, try to prevent your dog from getting bored or depressed. Provide him with more entertainment than usual – make his life fun!

Some dogs eat more when they are under stress. In this case you need to help him relax. Offer him a calm routine. Make sure he knows his position in the pack – the family – to help him feel secure. Hopefully, you always make it clear to him who is the leader.

Don't take it too personally if he doesn't readily submit to his new healthful eating routine straight away. He may try to blackmail you into feeding him more, by eating items of clothing or other undesirable objects.

The reduction in calories will have sharpened his brain, strengthened his determination and quickened his pace. So be extra careful about leaving food around.

Outside the home, you need to keep a strict watch on your dog. When visiting friends or relatives, for instance, he will try his complete repertoire of endearing tricks until they give him a titbit.

When you are out walking, your dog will constantly be on the lookout for something to eat. Food eaten outside the home is always much more appetising.

A week-old takeaway discarded in the gutter is a huge treat. At least the packaging provides a good source of dietary fibre.

Some dogs are allowed to go walkabout without their owners. There is little you can do in this case to stop him scavenging from rubbish tips and so forth. A desperate dog is not a pretty sight.

His instinct to hunt may be re-activated by his hunger. If you live in the country or near a park, he may come home with a freshly-caught rabbit, or something even bigger.

You may need to ground, even punish,
your dog in these circumstances.

In this case you will need to make sure
that he has plenty of supervised exercise.

Chapter Three

Your dog and exercise

Often lack of exercise is not the dog's fault. He may be kept inside all day while his owners are out, and there is only so much activity he can do at home alone.

Dogs should be taken for a long walk at least twice a day. The exact length of the walk depends upon the breed of the dog.

You will know when you have walked
him enough because he will be tired
when he gets home. . .

. . . and so will you. . .

If you're not that keen on long walks, learn the tricks by which the dog gets more exercise than you do. 'Fetch' is the best one. Throwing a stick or ball is good – but there are even better methods. . .

Watching him swim in the pond or river
is another – swimming is excellent fat-
burning exercise. But the water can be
cold.

Most larger dogs will enjoy
accompanying you while you hack out on
your horse.

Only obedient dogs should be exercised while you are on a bicycle. And avoid this method if you live in hilly country.

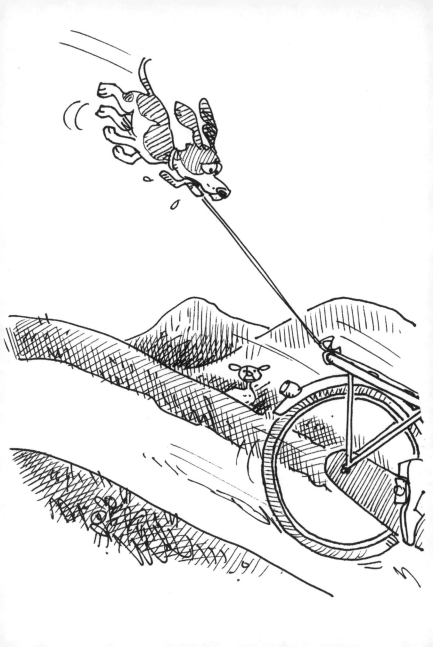

Some dogs are quite happy to walk on a treadmill. Be careful not to set the speed too high.

Avoid allowing your dog to chase
members of the opposite sex to get his
quota of calorie-burning. This could lead
to problems.

If your dog is lazy, he may try various tricks to avoid walking, once out. He may refuse to put one leg in front of the other, or even refuse to stand up at all.

Don't let your dog blackmail you into giving him an easy time of it.

But don't demand too much of your dog too quickly. If he is unfit you will need to very gradually increase the pace and distance of his walks. Taking him off the lead in the park will encourage him to run around more as he follows exciting trails.

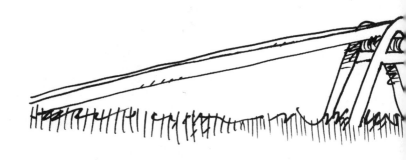

He may become more willing to exercise
if you add variety to his fitness routine.
Agility training classes are good both
mentally and physically.

They will help turn the most unfit, unwilling pet into a superb athlete who loves to. . .

. . . run. . .

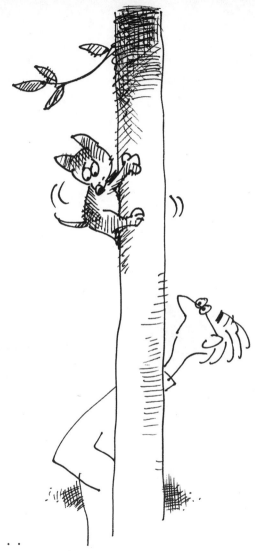

. . . climb. . .

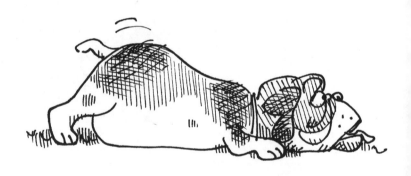

. . . crawl. . .

. . . and jump.

If your dog needs more walking than you can provide, enlist the services of a Dog Walker. Try to ensure that the walker walks dogs of roughly the same size as

yours and that he
doesn't try to walk too many at a time.
Otherwise, there could be problems.